THE COVENANT EXPERIENCE

Eleven Steps to a Better Marriage

Bob & Irene Tomonto
Myrna Gallagher

Resource Publications, Inc.
San Jose, California

Editorial director: Kenneth Guentert
Managing editor: Elizabeth J. Asborno

Reprint Department
Resource Publications, Inc.
160 E. Virginia Street #290
San Jose, CA 95112-5876

Library of Congress Cataloging in Publication Data
Tomonto, Bob, 1932-
    The covenant experience : eleven steps to a better marriage / Bob & Irene Tomonto, Myrna Gallagher.
        p.   cm.
    Includes bibliographical references.
    ISBN 0-89390-326-4
    1. Marriage—Religious aspects—Christianity. 2. Covenants—Religious aspects—Christianity. 3. Marriage—Religious aspects—Catholic Church.
4. Covenants—Religious aspects—Catholic Church. 5. Catholic Church—Membership. I. Tomonto, Irene, 1935- . II. Gallagher, Myrna, 1937- . III. Title.
    BV835.T65 1995
    248.4'82—dc20   95-5136

Printed in the United States of America

99 98 97 96 95 | 5 4 3 2 1

To Bishop Agustin A. Roman,
Auxiliary Bishop of the Archdiocese of Miami,
who recognized the need for a new tool
to assist couples in improving their marriages
and encouraged the authors to develop the Covenant Experience.

CONTENTS

PART TWO
Follow-Up Small-Group Meetings

ACKNOWLEDGMENTS

The authors are pleased to acknowledge the assistance of Manuel Carvajal, Gary & Kay Aitchison, Bob & Anne Tomonto, and the many couples who participated in the Covenant Experience for their comments on this work.

✟ PREFACE

Some thirty-odd years ago, a priest in the diocese of Albany, New York, knocked on our door and invited us to join the Christian Family Movement. Little did we know that our simple "yes" would lead to a life-long ministry to marriage and family.

Through the years we have seen marriage change from a traditional, stable family unit to the mega-mix of family forms of today. We had long felt that a parish-based weekend for couples followed by extended support-group meetings was needed. When Bishop Agustin Roman, Auxiliary Bishop of the Archdiocese of Miami, challenged us to "do something" to help marriages, we were encouraged to act on our conviction.

With the help of Myrna Gallagher, who had created a successful weekend for women called the Emmaus Weekend, the Covenant Experience was born. We feel that it provides an opportunity for a couple to grow in self-awareness plus enjoy the continuity and community within a parish necessary to sustain a strong Christian marriage.

Although we developed the Covenant Experience within a Roman Catholic setting, we feel it is adaptable to any Christian group. We would be interested in any comments that would make future editions more ecumenical. Please share your experiences using the Covenant Experience in another Christian setting by writing to us in care of the publisher.

In using *Covenant Experience*, may your journey in faith enrich your marriage and bring you closer to the Lord, who lives in covenant with you.

Bob and Irene Tomonto

✝ PART ONE

The Covenant Weekend

✝ WELCOME

Welcome to the Covenant Weekend. We are happy that you have taken the time to jump off the merry-go-round of normal life to look at your most precious possession—your marriage. We know that it has been difficult for you to take this time, so the team will do everything it can to make it a pleasant, growth experience.

All of us have gone to school for many years to acquire skills, support ourselves and earn a living. Sometimes we take refresher courses or training to upgrade ourselves or learn new skills. The Covenant Weekend can be seen as a refresher course, a way of upgrading your skills in your most important vocation, your marriage.

Christian marriage is a vocation, and the Catholic Church considers it a sacrament. We live in a time when Christian marriages are not held in high regard by our society. It is more difficult to remain married today than it was in the times of our parents or grandparents because a stable marriage has become the exception rather than the norm. New skills are needed to cope with this instability. That is why the company of other couples who also are committed to improving their marriages is so important.

The following guidelines will help you get the most out of the weekend:

1. Relax! You will not be placed in a situation that is designed to make you feel uncomfortable. The weekend consists of a series of sharings by members of the team followed by periods in which you and your spouse have the opportunity to dialogue on aspects pertaining to your marriage.

2. The role of the team is to support and assist you. The team will not improve your marriage on this weekend. That is something only you and your spouse can do through dialogue, prayer, and reflection.

3. Do not anticipate what will happen next. Put yourselves in the presence of God and allow Him to take your problems, worries, and hopes into His hands. Take the sessions and exercises one at a time. If you run out of time on one exercise, come back and finish it up at the next available free moment.

4. If you have any special physical or dietary needs, please let the team know. The team will be more than happy to help you.

Now, sit back and enjoy the Covenant Experience.

 STEP 1

We Know Our Marriage Is Not Perfect

Prayer *Blessed Are You, Lord Our God,*
Who Crowns Marriage with Love and Affection

Women

Lord of love,
> we thank You for the numerous gifts
> of our married love.

With the wisdom of generosity
> laid open since creation,
> You have blessed the union of man and woman
> with deep beauty in the song of love.

A mystic melody of sacred unity
> arises when two hearts are fused as one
> in the love of the Eternal One.

Lord God, we thank You for this holy gift.

Men

Lord and Creator of life,
> Your loving union with Your people
> was sung by the ancients
> in symbols of wedding feasts and intimate unions.

No other vocation in life
> have You, Lord, so richly blessed
> by interlacing intimacy and affection
> in the sacred union of hearts and bodies.

Women

We who share this ministry of marriage
> must also share its heavy burdens.

But our moments of loving affection,
> so human and so holy,
> lighten our trials and nourish us day by day
> in our common journey to You,
> our Lord and Beloved.

Men

Lord,
> may the happiness of these times of tenderness
> be for us a sacrament
> of our future and endless unity
> with You, with each other, (with our children,)
> and with all Your holy saints and lovers.

All

Blessed are You, Lord our God,
> who crowns marriage with love and affection.
> Amen.

Scripture   Tobit 8:4-9

Presentation   A team couple discusses how every marriage can be improved and introduces the exercises to follow.

Resources   Rules for Dialogue

Before you and your spouse begin the Marital Inventory, take a few minutes to read the following Rules for Dialogue and discuss them. They provide a fair and objective way to discuss issues.

1. The most important part of a dialogue is listening. Give the other person your full attention so that you can understand what he/she is saying. Look at the other person to understand the feelings behind his/her words. Do not concentrate on what you are going to say next until the other person has completed talking.

2. When the other person has completely stated his/her feelings on a particular subject, summarize what you understand him/her to say. For example, you could say: "I understand that you feel...." Try to summarize what was said in one sentence.

3. Neither person should monopolize the conversation. When reviewing the Marital Inventory, alternate questions with your partner.

4. Remember that you are talking to your best friend. Be considerate of his/her feelings.

5. Feelings are neither good or bad. They express the way a person perceives a particular situation. Deal with the reasons behind the feelings.

6. Never let the sun set without resolving an argument. Kiss and make up. As a minimum, agree to discuss the issue further at a mutually agreed future time.

♥ What would you change in the Rules for Dialogue?

The Marital Inventory

The journey begins with an honest, realistic evaluation of your marriage as it is today. You should answer the questions based on your feelings, not what you think might be the right answer. Remember, feelings are not wrong. It is what you do with your feelings that can be wrong. If you repress your feelings, you are avoiding the possibility of honest sharing with your partner that may ultimately lead to growth in your marriage.

Answer each of the questions on the Marital Inventory by checking the "yes," "no" or "uncertain" columns. Use the "uncertain" column when you do not understand the question or when your feelings on the subject vary from time to time. After you have answered all the questions, sit down with your spouse in a quiet place and go on to the next section of this manual.

COVENANT WEEKEND MARITAL INVENTORY

Please ignore questions that are not applicable.

Interests and Activities

Yes No Uncertain

☐ ☐ ☐ 1. Do you share common interests?

☐ ☐ ☐ 2. Are you comfortable with the activities and/or amount of time your spouse spends separate from you?

☐ ☐ ☐ 3. Can you afford your spouse's leisure activities?

☐ ☐ ☐ 4. Do you ever take time just to relax?

☐ ☐ ☐ 5. Do you have enough leisure time together?

☐ ☐ ☐ 6. Do you think your spouse spends too much time watching TV and/or sports events?

☐ ☐ ☐ 7. Do you consider your spouse as your best friend?

☐ ☐ ☐ 8. Do you and your spouse date on a regular basis?

Religion and Philosophy

☐ ☐ ☐ 1. Do you agree that marriage is a life-long commitment?

☐ ☐ ☐ 2. Are there any conditions under which you would divorce your spouse?

☐ ☐ ☐ 3. Do you see Christ as a co-partner in your marriage?

☐ ☐ ☐ 4. Do you and your spouse disagree on major articles of faith?

☐ ☐ ☐ 5. Do you and your spouse agree that your children should have a religious education?

☐ ☐ ☐ 6. Do you provide for the religious education of your children?

☐ ☐ ☐ 7. Do you and your spouse go to church together?

☐ ☐ ☐ 8. Do your children go to church?

☐ ☐ ☐ 9. Do you pray together?

Covenant Weekend Marital Inventory (continued)

☐ ☐ ☐ 10. Do you pray with your family?

☐ ☐ ☐ 11. Do you think that your spouse spends too much time at church?

Role Adjustment

☐ ☐ ☐ 1. Do you find your life fulfilling?

☐ ☐ ☐ 2. Do you think that your spouse finds his/her life fulfilling?

☐ ☐ ☐ 3. Are you a workaholic?

☐ ☐ ☐ 4. Is your spouse a workaholic?

☐ ☐ ☐ 5. Do our professional goals interfere with our roles of husband and wife?

☐ ☐ ☐ 6. Are you happy with your work?

☐ ☐ ☐ 7. Do you think your spouse is happy with his/her work?

☐ ☐ ☐ 8. Are you satisfied with the distribution of household chores?

☐ ☐ ☐ 9. Do you do a fair share of work around the house?

☐ ☐ ☐ 10. Do you think your spouse does a fair share of work around the house?

☐ ☐ ☐ 11. Are you satisfied with your own educational level?

☐ ☐ ☐ 12. Are you satisfied with your spouse's educational level?

☐ ☐ ☐ 13. Do you and your spouse share the same goals and ambitions?

☐ ☐ ☐ 14. Do you think that the major decisions in your marriage are made jointly?

Personal Adjustment

☐ ☐ ☐ 1. Do you have an addiction to alcohol, drugs, overeating, gambling, etc.?

☐ ☐ ☐ 2. Does your spouse have an addiction to alcohol, drugs, overeating, gambling, etc.?

☐ ☐ ☐ 3. Do you need help in controlling your addiction?

☐ ☐ ☐ 4. Do you think your spouse needs help in controlling his/her addiction?

☐ ☐ ☐ 5. Do you try to control your spouse?

☐ ☐ ☐ 6. Do you knowingly play games to manipulate your spouse?

☐ ☐ ☐ 7. Do you think your spouse controls or manipulates you?

☐ ☐ ☐ 8. Can you control your temper?

☐ ☐ ☐ 9. Can your spouse control his/her temper?

☐ ☐ ☐ 10. Are you frequently moody or depressed?

☐ ☐ ☐ 11. Do you have strong opinions that could be considered prejudices?

☐ ☐ ☐ 12. Are there persons you strongly dislike?

☐ ☐ ☐ 13. Do your dislikes disturb the serenity of your home?

☐ ☐ ☐ 14. Do you think that your spouse always acts in a mature way?

☐ ☐ ☐ 15. Do you always act in a mature way?

☐ ☐ ☐ 16. Do you think your spouse is strongly influenced by others?

☐ ☐ ☐ 17. Do you think your life is boring?

☐ ☐ ☐ 18. Do you think your life is stressful?

Interpersonal Relationships

☐ ☐ ☐ 1. Do you trust your spouse when he/she is not with you?

☐ ☐ ☐ 2. Does your spouse trust you when he/she is not with you?

☐ ☐ ☐ 3. Do you think that your spouse communicates with you?

☐ ☐ ☐ 4. Do you think that you are listened to?

☐ ☐ ☐ 5. Are there things you would like to change about your spouse?

Covenant Weekend Marital Inventory (continued)

☐ ☐ ☐ 6. Are there things you would like to change about your children?

☐ ☐ ☐ 7. Do you like your spouse's family?

☐ ☐ ☐ 8. Does your spouse like your family?

☐ ☐ ☐ 9. Do you ever remain angry with your spouse for more than a day?

☐ ☐ ☐ 10. Do you ever feel rejected by your spouse?

☐ ☐ ☐ 11. Do you like your spouse's friends?

☐ ☐ ☐ 12. Does your spouse like your friends?

☐ ☐ ☐ 13. Do you share mutual friends?

☐ ☐ ☐ 14. Does your spouse have a good relationship with your children?

☐ ☐ ☐ 15. Do you like your children's friends?

☐ ☐ ☐ 16. Did your parents approve of your choice of a marriage partner?

☐ ☐ ☐ 17. Did your spouse's parents approve of you?

☐ ☐ ☐ 18. Do you think that your spouse shares his/her feelings with you?

☐ ☐ ☐ 19. Do you love your spouse more now than on the day you married him/her?

☐ ☐ ☐ 20. Do you ever surprise your spouse with a gift?

Finance

☐ ☐ ☐ 1. Do you ever quarrel about money?

☐ ☐ ☐ 2. Do you or your spouse spend more than you earn?

☐ ☐ ☐ 3. Is the person who manages the finances in your family doing a good job?

☐ ☐ ☐ 4. Do you and your spouse agree on whether or not a wife should work outside the home?

☐ ☐ ☐ 5. Do you think your spouse earns enough money?

☐ ☐ ☐ 6. Do you think you personally have adequate money to spend on your personal needs/clothes?

☐ ☐ ☐ 7. Is your spouse a compulsive shopper?

☐ ☐ ☐ 8. Are you a compulsive shopper?

☐ ☐ ☐ 9. Are material things and possessions very important to you?

☐ ☐ ☐ 10. Do you or your spouse spend money that the other thinks is foolhardy?

☐ ☐ ☐ 11. Do you and your spouse agree on long-term financial goals?

☐ ☐ ☐ 12. Do you think that you are able to save for long-term goals?

Children

☐ ☐ ☐ 1. Are you and your spouse in agreement on the number of children you should have?

☐ ☐ ☐ 2. Are you in agreement as to how your children are being raised?

☐ ☐ ☐ 3. Do your children play one parent against the other?

☐ ☐ ☐ 4. Do you and your spouse argue about your children?

☐ ☐ ☐ 5. Do you think that your spouse spends enough time with your children?

☐ ☐ ☐ 6. Do you think that your spouse spends too much time with your children?

☐ ☐ ☐ 7. Do you agree on methods of discipline for your children?

☐ ☐ ☐ 8. When your children have grown, will you and your spouse still have things in common?

☐ ☐ ☐ 9. Do you argue with your children?

☐ ☐ ☐ 10. Do you agree on the role of mother?

☐ ☐ ☐ 11. Do you agree on the role of father?

Sexuality

☐ ☐ ☐ 1. Are you satisfied with your sex life?

☐ ☐ ☐ 2. Do you and your spouse agree on methods of birth control?

Covenant Weekend Marital Inventory (continued)

☐ ☐ ☐ 3. Have you and your spouse reconciled your decisions on birth control with your church's teachings?

☐ ☐ ☐ 4. Do you think that your spouse grew up with a good attitude about sex?

☐ ☐ ☐ 5. Do you think that you grew up with a good attitude about sex?

☐ ☐ ☐ 6. Do you think that intercourse expresses love in your marriage?

☐ ☐ ☐ 7. Do you feel hurt when your spouse is not interested in intercourse?

☐ ☐ ☐ 8. Do you think your spouse is interested in intercourse too frequently without regard to your feelings?

☐ ☐ ☐ 9. Do you think that your spouse is comfortable with his/her sexuality?

☐ ☐ ☐ 10. Do you prefer intimacy that does not always lead to intercourse?

☐ ☐ ☐ 11. Do you find sexual intimacy embarrassing?

☐ ☐ ☐ 12. Do you think that there is romance in your marriage?

☐ ☐ ☐ 13. Do you feel loved?

☐ ☐ ☐ 14. Do you think that often there is too little romance and too much quick sex in your life?

☐ ☐ ☐ 15. Do you show affection by hugging and holding hands with your spouse daily?

Evaluation of the Marital Inventory

Once you complete the Marital Inventory, get together with your spouse in a quiet spot and review the Rules for Dialogue. Do you agree to use these rules or do you want to make changes or additions to them?

♥ What changes or additions have you and your spouse agreed to make to the Rules for Dialogue?

Now look at each of the questions of the Marital Inventory where either of you checked the "uncertain" column. Discuss the question until you can resolve whether the answer should be in the "yes" or "no" column. (Remember that there are no right or wrong answers.)

Look at each of questions you answered differently and discuss the feelings that led to the response. Remember that feelings are neither good nor bad; they merely reflect the reality that one sees in a situation.

After you have finished, make a list of areas in which you recognize there is a need for improvement, or in which you are in disagreement. Jointly choose the most important areas in which you, as a couple, will work to improve during this weekend. Some of you might identify one major area that will capture and demand your complete attention; others may prefer to identify two or three less important areas which can be improved. For example: My spouse and I agree that there is too little romance and too much quick sex in our marriage.

My spouse and I agree that the following areas need to be improved in our marriage:

Statement of the Area(s)
to be Improved (Priority Concerns)   **Rank**

A. _____   _____

B. _____   _____

C. _____   _____

D. _____   _____

If you do not have enough time to complete this exercise before you are called to finish the session, complete it before the next session.

Evening

Prayer   My Lord, this day is ending
           and with it the work week,
              a week of holy days filled with Your divine
                 Presence.

How can I ask You to gift me with this weekend
   unless I am grateful for all the gifts of life
   in this week that is ending?

(Pause.)

I desire to greet this weekend with freshness.
Come Lord and remove all the grime and sin
    of the day and week now ending.
With the lamp of truth,
    I carefully explore the passages of my heart.

(Pause and silently recall how you have contributed to making your marriage less than perfect.)

My Lord,
    like a watchful guard,
    I await the coming of a new day,
I am filled with trust for whatever awaits me in
    this weekend.
Nourished by that trust,
    I pray for my special intentions and those of my
    spouse.

(Pause and silently ask God's help to make your marriage better.)

May Your holy spirits stand guard over our sleep
    so that we may rest peacefully
    and rise with abounding hope.
Lord of day and night, of life and death,
    We place ourselves into Your holy hands.[1]

---

[1] Adapted from Hays, "Saturday Evening Prayer," 167.

Notes & Reflections

STEP 2

We Realize Only God Can Help Us

Song   The morning begins with group singing.

Prayer   **Leader**

Father, you have blessed our lives
   with the sacrament of marriage.
We call to you today
   to shower us with Your love
   so that we may be open to each other.
Continue to increase our love
   throughout the joys and sorrows of everyday life,
   and help us to grow in holiness all of our days.
Grant this through our Lord, Jesus Christ, your
      Son,
   who lives and reigns with you and with the Holy
      Spirit,
   one God for ever and ever.
Amen.

Psalm 100   **Women**

Make a joyful noise to the LORD, all the earth.
> Worship the LORD with gladness;
> come into his presence with singing.

Men

Know that the LORD is God.
> It is he that made us, and we are his;
> we are his people, and the sheep of his pasture.

Women

Enter his gates with thanksgiving,
> and his courts with praise.
> Give thanks to him, bless his name.

Men

For the LORD is good;
> his steadfast love endures forever,
> and his faithfulness to all generations.

Scripture   Matthew 22:35-40

Prayer   **All**

Our lives are like a dance with the Lord.

Sometimes the music plays slowly
> and sometimes it breaks into a polka,
> but you, Lord, are always there as our partner,
> leading us and keeping us in time to the music.

Sometimes we even step on your toes,
> but you only smile at our awkwardness,
> leading us ever onward in relationship with you.

Put your arms around us, Lord,
  so that, together with our spouse,
  we three may dance the dance of life.
Amen.

Presentation   A team couple discusses how only God can help our marriages.

Marital
Adjustment
   Time   (5 Minutes)

Did you complete the Marital Inventory and the evaluation exercise last evening? If not, start by sitting down with your spouse and completing it now. It is very important to complete that step before going further. If you are uncertain regarding what you should have done or need some help with the process, ask one of the team members to help you.

♥ If you completed the Marital Inventory and the evaluation exercise last evening, what aspects of this presentation apply to your life?

♥ How can God help us improve in the areas of our "Priority Concerns?"

Journaling From time to time it is important to stop and reflect on our spiritual and marital growth. You can do this by keeping a personal journal of your goals and aspirations. Return periodically to your journal to record your thoughts, dreams and plans so that you can measure your development. Your journal does not have to be anything elaborate; a notebook of some kind in which the pages will stay together will be sufficient. There is no need for neatness or correct spelling. The journal is for you, so make it your own.

In his book *Adventure Inward*, Morton Kelsey writes,

> as we dig wells into our inner beings through keeping some kind of record of these selves, we find that there is a living water within each of us (17).

This weekend we will provide you with an opportunity to begin journaling through a series of exercises following some of the talks. You may want to exchange portions of your journal with your spouse or you may decide that you will discuss the items without exchanging journals, whichever way you feel most comfortable.

A wise man once said, "An unreflected life is a life not worth living." Journaling gives you a chance to write down your feelings, goals, and aspirations. Through this process you can grow and measure your progress. In addition, sometimes it feels good to get something that has been bothering you on paper and out of your head so that you can think clearly about it.

The best way to journal is to sit down and just start to write. You do not need to think ahead. Just start the pen or pencil moving and let your subconscious do the rest. Get the easy things out first, then go deeper. The important thing is to keep writing for the allotted time. A blank space is given after each question; use it up.

Often, after the title of an exercise, you will see a number enclosed in parentheses. This is an estimate of the time you should spend on the exercise. If you see two numbers in parentheses, for example, (15/15), this means that you should spend about fifteen minutes doing the exercise, then spend another fifteen minutes discussing it with your spouse.

Questions (15/15)

♥ What does Jesus mean to me?

♥ What role does Jesus play in our marriage?

After you have completed the Marital Adjustment and the Journaling exercises, sit down in a quiet place with your spouse and discuss your answers and/or exchange books.

STEPS 3 and 4

We Review Our Lives and We Turn to God Unconditionally

Marriage
Prayer   Lord, help us to remember when we first met,
            and the strong love that you grew between us.
        Help us to see the best within each other
            and within each member of our family.
        Help us to find answers to our problems.
        Lord, help us to say kind and loving words,
            and make us humble enough to ask forgiveness
                of each other.
            We put our marriage in Your hands.
        Amen.

Presentation   A team couple reviews their lives and shows how
                they have turned to God.

Resources   Abraham Maslow's Hierarchy of Needs

All human beings share common needs and motivations. Psychologists have studied people's behavior and developed theories that seem to explain why we act as we do in some situations.

One of these theories was developed by Abraham Maslow. He believed that we normally seek satisfaction (and thus are motivated) through a sequence of needs. The upper-level needs (esteem and self-actualization) ordinarily have no motivating effect until the lower-level needs (physical and security needs) are satisfied. In other words, if you are hungry or frightened you can think of little else. Once these lower-level needs are met, you can move on to think about the needs of others and the need to grow in self-esteem and self actualization.

People can move up and down the hierarchy of needs at different times in their lives; for example, a self-actualized person can lose a spouse and fall back into a social-need level in search of love and acceptance. Or a financially stable person can lose his/her job or other sources of income and fall back into a physical-need level in search of the basic necessities of life.

The following diagram illustrates Maslow's hierarchy of needs.[1]

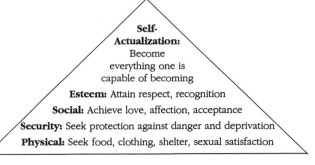

Self-Actualization: Become everything one is capable of becoming

Esteem: Attain respect, recognition

Social: Achieve love, affection, acceptance

Security: Seek protection against danger and deprivation

Physical: Seek food, clothing, shelter, sexual satisfaction

[1] Adapted from Haney 16.

Eight Steps to Improve Your Communications

1. Get to know yourself and your feelings. You cannot share your feelings unless you can be honest with yourself. Remember that feelings are neither right nor wrong. Having emotions and being able to express them is healthy.

2. Listen with your eyes and ears. The speaker's tone of voice and body language are as important as the words he/she is using.

3. Let your expression and posture show that you are listening attentively. Smiles, nods, and one-word responses help the other person express his/her feelings.

4. Try to understand what the other person is saying and identify the feeling being expressed. Summarize the message in your own words, such as, "I understand that you are saying...and that you feel...."

5. Try to place yourself in the other's place. Be compassionate and understanding.

6. Avoid providing temporary and/or instant solutions. It is important to address the situation and solve problems at their root, once and for all.

7. Let the other person express his/her feelings completely. Use this opportunity to understand, not to prepare your response.

8. Respond with love and tenderness for the other person.

Marital
Adjustment
Time (5 minutes)

Remember that the Marital Inventory is the most important tool you will use this weekend. Have you completed the Marital Inventory? Have you dialogued and established your "Priority Concerns?" If not, do so now *before* proceeding with the exericse below.

Keep in mind that you are trying to improve some aspects of your marriage that you identified through the Marital Inventory, that is, your "Priority Concerns."

♥ Has your family of origin exerted a negative influence on you in the areas that you have selected as "Priority Concerns?"

♥ How can you overcome this influence?

Journaling   Your life is important. You have a place, a value, a
             destiny which is unique; no one else has the same
             story. But beyond that, your story can help you
             reflect on where you have been and where you want
             to go. Does it not make sense to write your story?

**This second journaling exercise should be easier because
you have had some practice. Remember, the key is to start
writing and let the thoughts flow.**

Questions (15/15)

♥ What do you remember about your family life while growing up? Is the family you have formed with your spouse similar or different? How?

♥ Consider some period of change in your lives together. How was (is) God present during that change? Did you think of Him as "God and I" or as "God and We?"

After you have completed the Marital Adjustment and Journaling exercises, please sit down in a quiet place with your spouse and discuss the exercises and/or exchange books.

Notes & Reflections

✝ STEP 5

We See How Our Love Has Been Conditional

Prayer   *Blessing Prayer for Renewing a Commitment*
         Between Two Persons

Women

Holy Creator of love,
   we celebrate and renew our mutual lives
   that are lived as one.
We reseal, by this holy prayer,
   our commitment to each other,
   to a life of shared dreams, thoughts, and feelings.
We ask Your holy help
   so that we may be always awake
   to the needs of each other,
   needs both spoken and unspoken.
May our two but twin pathways
   lead us to the fullness of life
   and to You.

Men

We ask Your divine protection
    from the strong tides of daily troubles
    that tend to pull us apart from each other.
Shield us from the social sickness of no commitment.
Show us how to rechannel
    the hidden streams of selfishness
    that always threaten to separate us.
Lord, it was said by the ancients
    that from each of us flows a light
    that reaches straight to heaven;
    that when two persons destined to be united
        come together,
    their two streams fuse into a single bright beam
    reaching to heaven
    and giving splendor to all the universe.
We ask that our love for each other
    will shine as a single flame to all.

All

We thank You for the gifts of past years,
    as we place our hope in the ancient truth
    that whatever is begun here on earth
    will flower to fullness in heaven.
As a sign of our desire to be united,
    today and in the days to follow,
    we join now our hands as one
    and share a covenant
    with each other and with You, our Lord and God.
Amen.[1]

---

[1] Adapted from Hays, "Blessing Prayer for Renewing a Commitment Between Two Persons," 91.

Presentation   A team couple discusses how their love has been conditional.

Resources   Twelve Rules for Creative Conflicts

1. Choose a time and place comfortable for both of you. Do not fight when you have been drinking, have taken drugs, or are emotionally or physically stressed out.

2. Although it is all right to tell your children you disagree, do not argue or raise your voice to each other in their presence.

3. Choose your words carefully. Use precise language to say exactly what you mean. Remember that feelings are neither right nor wrong until they are acted upon.

4. Speak on an adult level. You are not accusing, or belittling, or calling the other person names. You are not talking as a parent would talk to a child. You are talking to a friend about a mutual problem.

5. Begin statements with the word "I." Avoid using "you," which accuses and blames.

6. Listen to the other person. Rephrase what he/she has said before answering (e.g., "I think you said...").

7. Remember that both of you come from different backgrounds and have different perspectives.

8. Focus on one problem at a time; do not dig up the past or confuse an issue by introducing other topics.

9. Do not bring in outsiders. Every time you tell someone else about "the problem," it

becomes bigger and more difficult to resolve.

10. Do not walk out. If the discussion becomes too difficult, take a break and start over shortly afterward.

11. Do not apologize just to end the discussion. Talk through your feelings until both understand the other person's point of view.

12. Reconcile your differences, forgiving each other and resolving to let the issues go.

Marital Adjustment Time (5 minutes)

Sometimes we let our love for our spouse become conditional, such as when we say, "I will do this if you do that."

♥ Could conditional love be the basic cause for problems identified as areas to work on from the Marital Inventory?

♥ How can I apply the principles discussed in this session to my marriage?

Journaling   There are many reasons for keeping a journal. If one is keeping a journal for inner growth, as a record of one's inner and outer life, or as a form of seeking help in dealing with pain, it may be necessary to write only as one concludes a sequence of steps, as is done here. A journal also can be used as an inner record, as a way of stimulating and deepening one's relationship with God. In this instance, it is crucial to keep a daily record, a daily journal.

Questions (15/15)

♥ How has my married love been conditional?

After you have completed the Marital Adjustment and Journaling exercises, sit down in a quiet place with your spouse and exchange books and/or discuss the exercises.

STEP 6

We Ask God to Heal Us

Marriage Prayer Lord, help us remember when we first met,
and the strong love that you grew between us.

Help us see the best within each other
and within each member of our family.

Help us find answers to our problems.

Lord, help us say kind and loving words,
and make us humble enough to ask forgiveness of
each other.

We put our marriage in Your hands.

Amen.

Presentation This talk asks God to heal us.

Marital Adjustment Time (5 Minutes)

Jesus forgave his most trusted friends after they had
abandoned him on Good Friday.

♥ Is there anything I could not forgive my
spouse?

♥ How can I apply the principles discussed in
this session to my marriage?

Journaling   A journal is a means whereby you can gather all of
yourself together to bring your total being before
God. When you trust Him enough to do this, God
begins to respond as the loving Father that He is.
Similarly, when you trust your spouse enough to
share your inner life with him/her, he/she can

respond with a welcome like that given the prodigal son (Lk 15:11-32).

Question (15/15)

♥ What positive steps can I make to change, stay away from sin, and become a better spouse?

The previous journaling exercises have sought to provide you with a tool to explore your own feelings and outlooks. This exercise will allow you to express your feelings to your spouse in the form of a "love letter." It may have been a long time since you wrote a love letter, or you may never have written one. Now is your chance to practice.

Write a love letter to your spouse, address the envelope provided, and seal the envelope with the letter enclosed. The team will mail the letter in a few weeks as a reminder of this weekend.

After you have completed the Marital Adjustment and Journaling exercises, please sit down in a quiet place with your spouse and exchange books and/or discuss the exercises.

If you have additional time, go back and review the previous exercises. Is there anything you did not finish? Do it now.

✝ STEP 7

We Commit to Marriage and Family

Prayer **Leader**

God our Father, You created man and woman
    to love each other in the bond of marriage.
Bless and support all of us, so that our marriages
    may become increasingly more perfect signs
    of the union between Christ and the Church.
We ask this through our Lord, Jesus Christ, your
    Son,
who lives and reigns with You and the Holy
    Spirit,
    one God, for ever and ever.
Amen.

Psalm 103[1] **Women**

Bless the LORD, O my soul,
    and all that is within me,
    bless his holy name.

---

[1] vv 1, 2, 8, 13, 17, 18

Men

Bless the LORD, O my soul,
  and do not forget all his benefits...

Women

The LORD is merciful and gracious,
  slow to anger and abounding in steadfast love.

Men

As a father has compassion for his children,
  so the LORD has compassion
    for those who fear him.

Women

But the steadfast love of the
    LORD is from everlasting to everlasting
  on those who fear him,
  and his righteousness to children's children,

Men

to those who keep his covenant
  and remember to do his commandments.

Amen.

Scripture   1 John 4:7-12

Prayer   Father, you have made the covenant bond of
      marriage
    a holy mystery,
    a symbol of Christ's love for the Church.
  With faith in You and in each other
    we pledge our love today.
  May our lives always bear witness
    to the reality of that love.

We ask this through our Lord Jesus Christ, your
    Son,
who lives and reigns with you and the Holy
    Spirit,
one God, for ever and ever.
Amen.

Presentation A team couples discusses their commitment to marriage and family.

Resources Marriage—A User's Guide:
The Six Stages of Marriage

See chart on the following two pages.

Marriage — A User's Guide:

STAGE	THEME	TASKS	ATTITUDES Toward Self/Others	AFFECTIVE Tone
1 Romance Honeymoon	Fusion	To nurture each other. To develop basis for satisfactory sex as well as caring/supportive relationship. To develop sense of belonging.	"We are one. We are the same. I need you." Partners give and receive with no effort.	Passionate. Romantic. Infatuation. "Madly in love." Lots of eye contact, touching.
2 Expectations	Compromise	To relinquish family of origin. To establish firm boundaries and self-esteem.	"You are changing. You are different. You hurt me. You are not living up to my expectations."	Disappointment. Anxiety. Conformity. Accommodation. Partners want to be close but don't know how to reach each other.
3 Power Struggle	Control	To begin developing problem-solving, decision-making, and negotiating procedures. To learn responsibility for own thoughts, feelings, actions. To support partner's growth as an individual.	"If you won't be like me I'll leave you."	Ambivalence. Distrust. Anger. Blaming. Polarization. Confrontation.
4 Seven-Year Itch (regardless of time married)	Competition	To develop individually and see partner as a separate person.	"Who am I? Can I make it without him/her? I want to be me."	Fight/flight. Argumentative/ Withdrawal.
5 Reconciliation	Cooperation	To develop a clearer sense of self. To understand the strivings for independence are normal. To take responsibility for individual needs. To develop more open, honest approach with partner, directly leading to increased intimacy.	"I am beginning to recognize my own inner struggles."	Reconciliation.
6 Acceptance	Collaboration	To stabilize perspective of self, partner. To choose to stay in relationship. To take responsibility for satisfying one's needs. To support partner's strengths and successes.	"I am seeing you as you are." Partners know themselves and enjoy being together.	Accepting. High level of warmth.

The Six Stages of Marriage

EXPECTATIONS Self/Other	PERCEPTIONS Self/Other	PROBLEMS	TRANSITION
"You will provide for my needs, wants, happiness."	"You are perfect." "You are mine. I am yours."	If one partner moves faster toward independence in providing for him/herself with job or friends, he/she may be pulled back by other, who may feel devastated the partner wants to do something with someone else.	Partners begin to recognize they are not exactly alike.
"You must make me happy." Closeness and dependence give way to the reality of household tasks.	"You are changing." "What's wrong with me?"	Problems may arise when partners are on different timetables in realizing they don't have to do everything together or feel the same all the time. One partner may feel rejected. Couple must work out how to be apart and still enjoy activities together. They must begin to find ways to reconcile their differentness.	Recognition and affirmation of differences.
"Why won't you make me happy?" Each partner has definite opinions about way partner should be. Each is afraid of giving in to other. "She's manipulative." "He won't see my position has validity."	"You are just like my mother/father. You don't love me. You are selfish, self-centered."	Power struggle can be intense. Partners get stuck in patterns of accusations and blame: "You always forget to..." "She always..." Both partners feel pain, distress.	Recognition of need to control. Begin taking independent/autonomous positions. Couple takes little steps to reconnect—they talk more. They make an effort to understand, try to acknowledge what the other is feeling: "I know you're feeling hurt but..." One partner may realize patterns tap into struggles with parents that were never resolved.
I can make myself happy. I can take care of myself. I need some time/space for myself.	I love myself.	Struggle for independence marks major change in marital relations. Some relationships will survive separation or divorce at this stage. One or both partners may begin distancing self from partner with an affair, turning outward and searching environment for partners rather than turning inward and completing self-identity process.	Recognition that each has individual needs to resolve. Recognition of own limitations. Stating wants/needs more openly. Can maintain one's own identity in the relationship. Partners choose to resolve issue of independence within the relationship.
Seeing self/other as real live separate person who may not meet one's expectations. Acceptance of the parts of self that create such expectations.	"You have your conflicts and I have mine. I can't change you; you can't change me."	Couple struggles toward intimacy. Partners may uncover unresolved conflicts from family of origin.	Use of conflicts and disagreements as opportunities for learning about selves. See differences as enhancement of relationship, rather than threat. Ups and downs are increasingly predictable.
"I'll take care of my needs and wants; you take care of yours."	We can be separate and we can reconnect without losing our identities. A time of surging personal growth; no need to pour energy into marriage.	Conflicts are handled as they arise, through negotiation.	Recognition and acceptance of interdependence.

Twelve Characteristics
of Happily Married Couples

1. Communicate effectively on a daily basis.

2. Pray together and share their faith with each other.

3. Make their spouse their best friend.

4. Share goals and aspirations, both personal and mutual.

5. Do not spend money they do not have.

6. Recognize that they come from different families, different backgrounds, and have been raised in different ways.

7. Share responsibility for tasks.

8. Deal with issues and let them go.

9. Do not try to change the other person. (The only person you can change is yourself.)

10. Understand the importance of romance and sex.

11. Commit to fidelity and permanence in marriage.

12. Feel that the other person is special.

Everybody has special needs. Add two other characteristics that would make your marriage happier:

1.

2.

Marital Adjustment Time (5 Minutes)

The six steps to a more perfect marriage investigated up to this session are designed to improve the relationship between you and your spouse. But your relationship is more than that. It is a relationship developed and, for some, blessed within the sacrament of marriage. It is a relationship in which you have pledged openness to children and family. The seventh step looks outward from the cozy relationship of the couple to other responsibilities.

♥ What does my marriage and family mean to me?

Journaling

Many couples and individuals have found that journaling has helped them get past their surface thoughts and dig deeper into the real reasons why they feel as they do and to examine their marriage, work and relationship with God. For those who wish to use this tool further, there are a number of fine books on the subject which are available in bookstores and public libraries (see References). These may help you more fully appreciate the usefulness of this tool.

♥ The thing I like best about journaling is:

Weekend Evaluation

Your help is needed to improve this weekend for other couples. Please fill it the Evaluation Form on the next two pages.

When you have finished with the evaluation form, tear it from your book and deposit it in the box designated by the team. Then, sit down in a quiet place with your spouse and discuss your reflections on the Characteristics of Happily Married Couples and the Marital Adjustment exercise.

EVALUATION FORM

We need your help in evaluating the effectiveness of the Covenant Weekend. Each person is asked to provide responses to the questions below. We do not need you to sign the form.

Respondent is: Male   Female (Circle one.)

Number of years married: _____

Children: Number_____ Ages_____

Please rate the following on a scale of 1 to 10 (10 being high):

_____ 1. Accommodations

_____ 2. Food

_____ 3. Effectiveness of the presentations

_____ 4. Usefulness of the Marital Inventory

_____ 5. Helpfulness of the journaling exercises

_____ 6. Prayer time

_____ 7. Saturday night party

Please circle "yes" or "no" in response to the following:

1. Do you feel that the weekend helped you and your spouse grow closer? Yes No

2. Do you plan to use the Marital Inventory as a checkup in the future? Yes No

3. Do you plan to use the journaling tool in the future? Yes No

4. Do you plan to use the 11-step method in the future? Yes No

5. Would you be interested in attending follow-up, small-group meetings to reinforce the ideas presented on the weekend?
Yes No

6. Would you recommend the weekend to your friends? Yes No

Evaluation Form (page 2)

Please answer the following:

1. What was the most important thing that you learned/experienced on the weekend?

2. What two (or more) things would you add to improve the weekend?

3. What would you change to make the weekend more effective?

4. Other comments?

Thank you. God bless your marriage and your families.
The Team

Where Do We Go from Here?

Marriage Prayer

Lord, help us remember when we first met
    and the strong love that you grew between us.
Help us see the best within each other
    and within each member of our family.
Help us find answers to our problems.
Lord, help us say kind and loving words,
    and make us humble enough to ask forgiveness
      of each other.
We put our marriage in Your hands.
Amen.

Throughout this weekend you have listened to presentations and worked on exercises alone and with your spouse. Now is the time to acknowledge that there is a community aspect of marriage beyond you and your spouse, namely your family and the community in which you live.

We live in a time of great mobility. Few of us still live where we were born. We often lack friends and relatives to whom we can relate and in whom we can find acceptance. A community of couples who think and feel as you do can help you grow in your marriage by giving you an opportunity to discuss the problems of raising a family in today's world and by sharing their experiences and solutions to problems of marriage and family. They can provide some of the support that in previous generations, and today in some cultures, was/is rendered by the extended family, a source of support that many people lack.

This exercise involves you interacting with other couples at your table. Do the following reflection together. Everybody has something to share, so give each person a chance to contribute. Appoint one of the persons at the table as a spokesperson to give a short summary report to the entire group at the end of the session.

Small-Group Exercise

When people try to define the word "family," they use terms like "home," "love," "children," "friends," "household," "closeness." When family therapists describe a family, they use the word "system," a word which encompasses many of the other concepts.

In a system, the whole is greater than the sum of its parts. A family viewed as a system is a group of individuals, each having his/her own life force, yet each having a specific function within the family. Family members act and interact on a daily basis; they live in relationship to one another; they have the power to affect others for better or worse.

The word "system" implies interdependence. Individual family members connect to one another both physically and emotionally. They are connected by the things they share and the things they do for one another; however, the most important connections are the feelings they have for one another.

A family system works only when its members share common goals. They must talk to one another. When they have problems, they must come together to heal them.

Discuss As a Couple (15 Minutes)

Thinking about our immediate family:

1. How are we doing?

2. What are our family strengths?

3. What are the weaknesses in our family?

Thinking about our parents, grandparents and other members of our extended family whose lives affect us:

1. How are we doing within our extended family?

2. What are the strengths of our extended family?

3. What are the weaknesses in our extended family?

Discuss As a Group (30 minutes)

1. What do we learn when we look at a family as a system?

2. How can problems with one family member affect the whole family? Feel free to give examples.

3. What can be done to bring families closer together?

Our best intentions and thoughts are incomplete unless they motivate us to apply them to our lives. We can begin to build a pattern of applying what we have discovered this weekend by resolving to change our lives in some small way. The following Application exercise will be a start in this process.

Application   Choose one of the following:

1. Plan a family meeting to discuss with your children "how well our family is doing."

2. Plan a special activity that celebrates how important each member of your family is to the family system. For example, gather around the dining room table, begin with one individual and have each person give one reason why that individual is important to your family. Then proceed around the table until everyone has been affirmed. End with a spontaneous prayer of thanksgiving.

♥ We plan to do the following activity as a family during the next week:

Reports One person from each table should summarize the group discussion of the three questions and report some of the applications planned by members of the group.

Presentation A team couple discusses options for follow-up small-group meetings.

Notes & Reflections

Closing Ceremony

Prayer   Father, we commemorate with joy your presence
in our life.
In that spirit we celebrate the gift of your
sacrament of marriage,
in the name of the Father,
and of the Son,
and of the Holy Spirit.
Amen.

Scripture   Ruth 1:16-17

But Ruth said,

Do not press me to leave you
or to turn back from following you!
Where you go, I will go;
Where you lodge, I will lodge;
your people shall be my people,
and your God my God.
Where you die, I will die—
there will I be buried.
May the LORD do thus and so to me,
and more as well,
if even death parts me from you!"

Song

Sing "The Wedding Song" or another appropriate song.

Renewal of Vows

Couples join hands and repeat:

Men

I, (name), take you, (name), to be my wife.
  I promise to be true to you
  in good times and in bad,
  in sickness and in health.
I will love you and honor you all the days of my
  life.

Women

I, (name), take you, (name), to be my husband.
  I promise to be true to you
  in good times and in bad,
  in sickness and in health.
I will love you and honor you all the days of my
  life.

Each couple comes forward. Each spouse pours wine or juice/soda from an individual cup or pitcher into a third, empty cup, which they take to their table. When all the couples have filled their cups, both spouses drink from the third cup as a symbol that two have become one.

Nuptial Blessing

Let us pray to the Lord.

Holy Father, You created humankind in Your own
  image

and made man and woman to be joined as
husband and wife
in union of body and heart
and to fulfill their mission in this world.

Father, to reveal the plan of Your love,
You made the union of husband and wife
an image of the covenant between You and Your
people.
In the fulfillment of this sacrament
the marriage of Christian man and woman
is a sign of the marriage between Christ and the
Church.
Father, stretch out Your hand, and bless everyone
here.

Lord, grant that, as they live this sacrament,
they may share with each other the gifts of Your
love
and become one in heart and mind
as witnesses to Your presence in their marriage.
Help them create a home together.

Give Your blessing to Your daughter
so that she may be a good wife and mother
caring for the home, faithful in love for her
husband, generous and kind.
Give Your blessing to Your son
so that he may be a faithful husband and a good
father.

Father, grant that,
as they come together to Your table on earth,
so they may one day have joy of sharing Your
feast in heaven.
We ask this through Christ our Lord.
Amen.

Witnesses
(Optional)

At this time, some couples may wish to share their feelings about the Covenant Experience.

✝ PART 2

Follow-Up
Small-Group
Meetings

 STEP 8

We Review
Our Progress

Prayer *Blessed Are You, Lord Our God,*
Who Crowns Marriage with Love and Affection

Lord of love,
    we thank You for the numerous gifts of our
    married love.
With the wisdom of generosity
    laid open since Creation,
You have blessed the union of man and woman
    with deep beauty in the song of love.
A mystic melody of sacred unity
    arises when two hearts are fused as one
    in the Love of the Eternal One.
Lord God, we thank You for this holy gift.
Amen.

The leader couple should ask someone to read the Reflection below. Then let the couples find a private spot in the meeting area to do the section entitled Discuss Privately As a Couple. Each individual should take about ten minutes to write his/her responses to the questions and then get together with his/her spouse to discuss their individual reponses for about ten minutes. The group should then come back together to do the exercise entitled Discuss As a Group. The meeting will be most effective if couples review the matierial together before the meeting.

Reflection   The Catholic Church held an ecumenical council known as Vatican II from 1962-65, which became a rich source of teaching on marriage and family. In the "Pastoral Constitution on the Church in the Modern World" (*Gaudium Et Spes*), the Church Fathers of Vatican II describe the Christian family as a reflection of the loving covenant uniting Christ with the Church (Eph 5:32). Through "the love of the spouses; their fruitfulness; their solidarity and faithfulness; and by the loving way in which members of the family work together" (48), this covenant is demonstrated to others. The couple and the entire family become a sign of the sacrament of matrimony.

These are high ideals for any family. We are imperfect people living with others in an imperfect world. There are many forces that complicate our relationships, that undermine our marriages, including personal needs, family and job pressures, social and financial worries, and the constant tug of a very secular society.

Only in Christ can we meet the challenge of marriage today. Only in Christ can we live in a covenant relationship.

Discuss Privately As a Couple (10/10)

During the Covenant Weekend you began to follow the eleven steps to a more perfect marriage. Step 8 is an opportunity to review your progress and make any changes, if required. Take a few minutes now to review the first seven steps and see how they relate to your marriage.

1. We know our marriage is not perfect.

2. We realize only God can help.

3. We review our lives.

4. We turn to God unconditionally.

5. We see how our love has been conditional.

6. We ask God to heal us.

7. We commit to marriage and family.

Looking once more at the Marital Inventory and recalling the areas we decided to improve:

♥ How are we doing?

♥ Do we need more time?

♥ Do we need help from someone outside our family?

♥ Are we ready to move on to another area?

Discuss As a Group (45 minutes):

1. What did we gain from the weekend?

2. What do we think the Church Fathers are telling us about Christian marriage?

3. What specific things can couples do to improve their marriage and family life?

4. What specific things can couples do to improve their relationship with the Lord?

Reports (5 minutes)

Were you able to complete the actions decided upon in the Application section of the last session of the weekend? What were the results?

Application   Before the Next Meeting (20 minutes)

Looking at your marriage and family, choose one specific thing that you can do in the next week to improve the quality of your married life. This may be a personal or a group activity.

♥ During the next week we will:

Preparation for Step 9

Date:

Time:

Place:

Prayer for the Family

Heavenly Father, You have given us a model of life in the Holy Family of Nazareth.

Help us, O Loving Father, to make our family another Nazareth where love, peace, and joy reign.

May it be deeply contemplative, intensely Eucharistic and vibrant with joy.

Help us to stay together in joy and sorrow through family prayer.

Teach us to see Jesus in the members of our family, especially in their distressing disguise.

May the Eucharistic Heart of Jesus make our hearts meek and humble like His and help us to carry out our family duties in a holy way.

May we love one another as God loves each one of us more and more each day, forgive each other's faults as You forgive our sins.

Help us, O Loving Father, to take whatever You give and to give whatever You take with a big smile.

Immaculate Heart of Mary, cause of our joy, pray for us.

St. Joseph, pray for us.

Holy Guardian Angels, be always with us, guide and protect us.

Amen.

✝ STEP 9

We Seek the Lord in Prayer

Prayer   Our Father, who art in heaven,
   hallowed be thy name.
Thy kingdom come, thy will be done
   on earth as it is in heaven.
Give us this day our daily bread,
   and forgive us our trespasses
   as we forgive those who trespass against us,
   and lead us not into temptation,
   but deliver us from evil.
For yours is the kingdom, the power and the
   glory, now and forever.
Amen.

Scripture   Tobit 8:4-8

   ...Tobias got out of bed and said to Sarah, "Sister,
   get up, and let us pray and implore our Lord that
   he grant his mercy and safety." So she got up,
   and they began to pray and implore that they
   might be kept safe. Tobias began by saying,

"Blessed are you, O God of our
ancestors,
and blessed is your name in all
generations for ever and ever.
Let the heavens and the whole
creation bless you forever.

You made Adam, and for him
you made his wife Eve
as a helper and support.
From the two of them the
human race has sprung.
You said, 'It is not good that the
man should be alone;
let us make a helper for him
like himself.'
I now am taking this kinswoman
of mine,
not because of lust,
but with sincerity.
Grant that she and I may find
mercy
and that we may grow old together."

And they both said, "Amen, Amen."

Tobias and Sarah began their marriage with prayer. We too must seek the Lord in prayer as we call on the gift of grace to bless our relationship to our spouse and to our family.

Ways to Pray

There are many different ways to pray. From traditional, memorized prayers to less traditional forms like charismatic prayer, each person must take the first step in his/her journey of faith. For married couples it is good to emulate Tobias and Sarah and explore the concepts of couple prayer. Beyond this, each family is called to a family spirituality lived amid the daily routine of spilled milk and lost homework. In his book *When God Is at Home with Your Family*, David Thomas writes:

> For me spirituality refers to the meshing in daily life of a set of deep relationships.... [P]rimary in importance is the relation with God, who is experienced not as outside of life, but as a real, personal presence active and living in the lives of each family member. Joined to the relation with God are the human relations of husband/wife and parent/child....How the family members live together in that divine presence is what constitutes family spirituality.

> In one sense the spirituality of the family is the sum of the spiritual lives of the individual members. Each person's life is very important, but Christian family life is more than that sum....There is a synergistic process at work in family life. This means that the total effect of life together is more than the sum of its parts. It is the shared life of the family that forms the heart of family spirituality (6).

Discuss Privately As a Couple (10/10)

♥ How important is prayer in our lives? In the life of our family?

♥ Do we feel we are growing in spirituality?

♥ What might we do to improve the quality of prayer life of our family?

Discuss As a Group (60 minutes)

1. What were the traditions of prayer in our family of origin?

2. What "helps" to improve our prayer life are available in the parish?

3. How important is it to have a Spiritual Director? How would someone find a Spiritual Director in our community? (A Spiritual Director can be a priest, deacon, minister, religious, lay person or couple who have a mature spirituality and special training to lead others to deeper faith life.)

4. What suggestions do we have to help improve the prayer life of children? Of teenagers? Of young adults? Of marginal believers?

Reports (5 minutes)

Report on what you did since the last meeting to improve the quality of your family life.

Application Before the Next Meeting (20 minutes)

Plan an action which will help your family know and love Jesus more. Start by asking your children what they would like to do and involve them in the preparation and implementation. Examples might be to read scripture passages together and discuss them; to pray together as a family; to celebrate a seder meal during Holy Week; to light and pray the Advent wreath.

♥ During the next week we will:

Preparation for Step 10

Date:

Time:

Place:

The group is only as effective as its individual members. Each couple should accept responsibility for the group. They should understand that their participation is necessary. Plan to come on time, share your ideas, and apply each step to your marriage and family. Go back and review the Marital Inventory and the previous steps with your spouse between meetings. Pray.

Closing

Prayer

Compose your own spontaneous prayer starting with "Blessed are You, Lord our God, who...." Start with one individual and go around the group. End with an "Our Father."

You can also use this format in your family prayers.

We Make Our Home a Domestic Church

Lord our God
may Your divine name be always holy within our
home.
May You, as Holy Father and Divine Mother,
lovingly care for all who shall live here.
May Your kingdom come in this home
as we love and respect one another.
May we always do Your holy will
by living in harmony and unity.
May we never suffer from lack of bread,
from a lack of all that we need
to nourish our family.
May the spirit of pardon and forgiveness reside
with us
and be always ready to heal our divisions.
May the spirits of mirth and laughter, hope and
faith,

playfulness and prayer, compassion and love
be perpetual guests in our home.

May our door be always open to those in need.
Open be this door
to the neighbor or to the stranger.

May our friends
who come to us in times of trouble and sorrow,
find our door open to them and to their needs.

May the holy light of God's presence
shine forth brightly for all who shall live here
and for everyone who shall come to this door.

May God's holy blessing rest upon us all,
in the name of the Father,
and of the Son,
and of the Holy Spirit.

Amen.

Reflection   When most people think of a church, they think of
a building with pews and an altar. In the documents
of Vatican II, the Catholic Church teaches about a
different kind of church—the church of the home.
They call this the "domestic church."

In the "Decree on the Apostolate of the Laity" is
written:

> The family has received from God its mission to
> be the first and vital cell of society. It will fulfill
> this mission if it shows itself to be the Domestic
> Sanctuary of the Church through the mutual
> affection of its members and the common prayer
> they offer to God, if the whole family is caught
> up in the liturgical worship of the church, and if
> it provides active hospitality and promotes justice
> and other good works for the service of all the
> brethren in need (11).

How do we do this? How do we make our home a
domestic church? In his book *Households of Faith,*

David Thomas lists five practices toward this end (6-13). These practices deal with the following:

1. Family table

Mealtime is the one time of the day when the whole family should gather together. It can be a positive time of communication, understanding, and worship.

2. Family prayers

Conversation with God is an important part of the life of the Christian family. Whether at mealtime or bedtime, whether formal or spontaneous, prayer is important to a family. Fr. Patrick Payton, a promoter of family prayer, used the phrase, "The family that prays together, stays together."

3. Family time

Every family should plan quality time together. Make these fun times and also times to discuss anything that family members want to bring up.

4. Family memories

Every family has a history and needs a set of traditions to pass from one generation to another. Plan how to discover and celebrate the history of your family. Create new traditions.

5. Family dreams

A family must move into the future by planning and dreaming what it can do together. Family calendars, vacation plans, outreach activities of service to others, and plans for life choices are all subjects for family dreaming.

Discuss Privately As a Couple (10/10)

♥ Where did I get my basic Christian values? From my parents, church, or school?

♥ Where do I get my ability to relate to others—to love, trust and forgive?

♥ Looking at our own family, do we have family meals together? family prayer? family time? family memories and traditions? family dreams?

Discuss As a Group (60 minutes)

1. Do I think that meals together, prayer, sharing time, memories, traditions, and dreams as a family are important? Why?

2. Why is it so hard to think of my family as church? How can runny noses, dirty diapers, and cluttered kitchens have anything to do with the "people of God" or the "body of Christ?"

3. Why does Vatican II use terms such as "mutual affection," "common prayer," "hospitality," and "service to others" in relation to families? Are these important in a family?

4. Is my home is a domestic church?

Reports (5 minutes)

What did you do to introduce family prayer in your home?

Application Before the Next Meeting (20 minutes)

Develop a plan with your spouse to make your home a more perfect domestic church.

♥ We will make our home a domestic church by:

Preparation for Step 11

Date:

Time:

Place:

Look ahead to Step 11 and plan a time to review the questions listed in the section called Discuss with Your Family. Hold a family meeting and be prepared to report on your family's responses at the next meeting.

Closing

Prayer

Heavenly Father,
look on us, Your people,
and show us the vision of Your great love for us.
Help us to be a people of courage,
a gentle people, who dare to love,
who know how to share,
and who live together in faith,
both in ourselves and in You.
May our family life be a sign of Your presence in
the world.
We ask this in the name of Jesus, our brother,
and of the Spirit, our strength.
Amen.[1]

---

[1] *Rooted in Faith* inside front cover.

Notes & Reflections

✝ STEP 11

We Reach Out
to Other Families

Prayer for the Family   Heavenly Father, You have given us a model of
life in the Holy Family of Nazareth.

Help us, O Loving Father, to make our family
another Nazareth where love, peace, and joy
reign.

May it be deeply contemplative, intensely
Eucharistic and vibrant with joy.

Help us to stay together in joy and sorrow
through family prayer.

Teach us to see Jesus in the members of our
family, especially in their distressing disguise.

May the Eucharistic Heart of Jesus make our
hearts meek and humble like His and help us
to carry out our family duties in a holy way.

May we love one another as God loves each one
of us more and more each day,
forgive each other's faults as You forgive our sins.

Help us, O Loving Father, to take whatever You
　　give and to give whatever You take
　with a big smile.

Immaculate Heart of Mary, cause of our joy,
　　pray for us.
St. Joseph, pray for us.
Holy Guardian Angels, be always with us,
　　guide and protect us.
Amen.

Reflection　A popular song a few years ago said, "Love isn't love 'til you give it away!" This would be a good motto for families. Families who love one another are challenged to spread that love to others.

The call to serve others is the eleventh step in the process of creating a more perfect marriage and family. This is the perfection of love—the love of God, the love of spouse, the love of neighbor.

How do I serve others? In the Gospel according to Matthew (25:34-40), Jesus tells us about the last judgment and the criteria that will be used to select the blessed:

> "Then the king will say to those at his right
> hand, 'Come, you that are blessed by my Father,
> inherit the kingdom prepared for you from the
> foundation of the world; for I was hungry and
> you gave me food, I was thirsty and you gave
> me something to drink, I was a stranger and you
> welcomed me, I was naked and you gave me
> clothing, I was sick and you took care of me, I
> was in prison and you visited me.' Then the
> righteous will answer him, 'Lord, when was it
> that we saw you hungry and gave you food, or
> thirsty and gave you something to drink? And
> when was it that we saw you a stranger and
> welcomed you, or naked and gave you clothing?
> And when was it that we saw you sick or in
> prison and visited you?' And the king will answer

them, 'Truly I tell you, just as you did it to one of the least of these who are members of my family, you did it to me.'"

Discuss with Your Family

Prior to the meeting, discuss the following questions with your whole family.

♥ Who are the least of our brothers? Who are the strangers in our midst? What are their needs?

♥ What are we doing to help others as individuals? as a family?

♥ What might we do to help others in a more positive way?

Report on Family Meetings (20 minutes)

Each couple summarizes the results of their family meeting.

Discuss As a Group (75 minutes)

1. Reflecting on stories in our local newspapers, what are the needs of the people in our community?

2. How can we, as couples, develop a sense of social responsibility?

3. What can parents do to help their children develop a sense of social responsibility?

You have completed the last step of the eleven-step process to improve your marriage. Please contact the team coordinating couple to find out if they are planning a reunion of the couples who participated in the Covenant Weekend. If a general reunion is not planned, schedule The Next Step in this book.

Application — Within the Next Week (20 minutes)

Choose one of the following:

1. Plan one positive action that increases your social awareness, and invite your family to come along. For example, you might choose to volunteer at a local soup kitchen, or invite another family, or maybe a foreign student, to your home for a holiday meal. Use your imagination and do something that is right for your family.

2. Read *Parenting for Peace and Justice* by Kathleen and James McGinnis. The authors have developed several strategies for teaching social responsibility to children and leading a network of families striving to live the gospel message.

♥ We plan to involve our family in the following outreach project:

Preparation for The Next Step

Date:

Time:

Place:

Marriage Prayer

Lord, help us remember when we first met
   and the strong love that you grew between us.
Help us see the best within each other
   and within each member of our family.
Help us find answers to our problems.
Lord, help us say kind and loving words,
   and make us humble enough to ask forgiveness
      of each other.
We put our marriage in Your hands.
Amen.

Present petitions for your family concerns. End with an "Our Father."

The Next Step

Marriage
Prayer
Lord, help us remember when we first met
and the strong love that you grew between us.
Help us see the best within each other
and within each member of our family.
Help us find answers to our problems.
Lord, help us say kind and loving words,
and make us humble enough to ask forgiveness
of each other.
We put our marriage in Your hands.
Amen.

Reflection
[T]he basic vocation of every person, whether
married or living a celibate life, is the same:
"Follow the way of love, even as Christ loved
you" (Eph. 5:2). The Lord issues this call to your
family and to every family regardless of its
condition or circumstances.

Love brought you to life as a family. Love
sustains you through good and bad times. When
our church teaches that the family is an "intimate
community of life and love," it identifies
something perhaps you already know and offers
you a vision toward which to grow.

What you do in your family to create a community of love, to help each other to grow, and to serve those in need is critical not only for your own sanctification, but for the strength of society and our church. It is a participation in the work of the Lord, a sharing in the mission of the Church. It is holy (excerpted from "Follow the Way of Love: Pastoral Message to Families, by the U.S. Catholic Bishops" [November 1993]).

Discuss Privately As a Couple (15/15)

♥ How are we doing in improving our marriage?

♥ What is different in our marriage now compared to the time prior to the Covenant Experience?

After reviewing your Marital Inventory, answer the following:

♥ How are we doing?

♥ Do we need more time?

♥ Do we need help from someone outside of our family?

♥ Are we ready to move on to another area?

Discuss As
a Group (45 minutes)

1. How has the Covenant Experience helped us to create a "community of love"?

2. Couples who complete the Covenant Experience are often eager to continue meeting in this format. A small group provides an opportunity to meet with other couples and parents to discuss concerns, envision dreams, and celebrate family. It provides a natural support system in times of need and special friendship with others who share the same expectations of Christian marriage. Are we interested in continuing to meet in small groups, using new materials? Are we interested in working together in some other form of marriage ministry? See Resources below.

Resources The Christian Family Movement

The CFM is the best follow-up program for the Covenant Experience; in fact *The Covenant Experience* was written with CFM in mind.

A CFM group consists of six to eight couples and a chaplain who meet every two weeks to study scripture, discuss topics of interest to couples and families, and take actions to change the quality of their lives and the lives of their families and friends. They use one of many inquiry programs that are available, ranging from parenting and marriage programs to material on outreach and social justice issues.

Through this ecumenical network of friends, the individual person finds acceptance and faith. Beyond this network, both husband and wife find the basis for their on-going relationship and the opportunity to work together on projects of shared interests. They learn to combine their talents in a supportive way and to grow in their faith experience, especially their love for Jesus and for each other.

For more information contact:

The Christian Family Movement
National Office
Box 272
Ames, Iowa, 50010
515-232-7432

Family Intercommunications, Relationships, Experiences, Services, Inc.

FIRES is the parent organization of the Marriage Encounter Movement and the brainchild of Fr. Gabriel Calvo. Their materials include the following program manuals:

1. *Self-Encounter at Home*

2. *Marriage Encounter at Home*

3. *Family Encounter at Home*

4. *Personal Retorno at Home* (reconciliation with God — personal)

5. *Marriage Retorno at Home* (reconciliation with God — couple)

6. *Family Retorno at Home* (reconciliation with God — whole family)

For more information contact:

FIRES, INC.
1425 Otis Street, NE
Washington, D.C.m 20017
202-526-5977

Teams of Our Lady

Meeting in small groups once a month, they follow a program dealing with prayer, scripture, and marriage. For additional information contact:

Teams of Our Lady
140 W. Main St.
Harbor Springs, Michigan, 49740
616-526 9000

Marriage Ministry

Many couples choose to share what they have gained through the Covenant Experience by following one of several marriage ministry options:

1. Contacting the pastor of a neighboring parish and offering to initiate the Covenant Experience for that community.

2. Contacting the Family Life Office in your diocese and volunteering to help in the Engaged and/or Marriage Ministry programs.

3. Volunteering to work in the Engaged and Family Life programs in the parish.

Closing   Compose your own spontaneous prayer starting with "We ask You, Lord...." End with the "Our Father."

Notes & Reflections

✝ REFERENCES

General   Barbeau, Clayton C. *Joy of Marriage*. Minneapolis: Winston, 1976.

Burtchaell, James. *For Better For Worse: Sober Thoughts on Passionate Promises*. New York: Paulist, 1985.

Buscaglia, Leo. *Living, Loving & Learning*. New York: Ballantine, 1982.

———. *Love*. New York: Ballantine, 1972.

———. *Loving Each Other*. New York: Ballantine, 1984.

Carlinsky, Dan. *Do You Know Your Wife?* Los Angeles: Price, Stern and Sloan, 1984.

Chapin, Alice. *Four Hundred Ways To Say I Love You*. Wheaton, Ill.: Tyndale House, 1981.

Curran, Dolores. *Stress and the Healthy Family*. New York: HarperCollins, 1993.

———. *Traits of a Healthy Family*. New York: Ballantine, 1983.

Finley, Mitch. *Your Family in Focus*. Notre Dame: Ave Maria, 1989.

Foley, Gerald. *Courage to Love: When Your Marriage Hurts*. Notre Dame: Ave Maria, 1992.

Gottman, John. *Why Marriages Succeed or Fail*. New York: Simon & Schuster, 1994.

Hayes, Bernard. *Love in Action: Reflections on Christian Service*. Locust Valley, NY: Living Flame Press, 1985.

Hays, Edward. *Prayers for the Domestic Church*. Easton, Kansas: Forest of Peace Books, 1979.

Kenny, James. *Loving and Learning: A Guide to Practical Parenting*. Cincinnati: St. Anthony Messenger Press, 1988.

Leiperet, Jack, and William Rabior. *Marriage Makers, Marriage Breakers: Counseling for a Stronger Relationship*. Ligouri: Liguori, 1990.

Livingston, Patricia. *Lessons of the Heart*. Notre Dame: Ave Maria Press, 1992.

Martin, Ralph. *Husbands, Wives, Parents, Children: Foundations for the Christian Family*. Ann Arbor: Servant Books, 1978.

McGinnis, James and Kathleen. *Parenting for Peace and Justice*. Maryknoll, New York: Orbis, 1981.

Powell, John. *Happiness Is an Inside Job*. Allen, Tex.: Tabor, 1989.

―――. *The Secret of Staying in Love*. Allen, Tex.: Argus Communications, 1974.

―――. *Through Seasons of the Heart*. Allen, Tex.: Tabor Publishing, 1987.

―――. *Unconditional Love*. Allen, Tex.: Argus Communications, 1978.

―――. *Why Am I Afraid to Love?* Allen, Tex.: Argus Communications, 1972.

Reilly, Christopher. *Making Your Marriage Work*. Mystic, Conn.: Twenty-Third Publications, 1989.

Roberts, Challon. *Partners in Intimacy: Living Christian Marriage Today*. Mahwah, New Jersey: Paulist, 1988.

Rooted in Faith. Ames, Iowa: Christian Family Movement, 1990.

Sanford, John. *Between People: Communicating One-to-One*. New York: Paulist, 1982.

Smalley, Gary. *Joy That Lasts*. Grand Rapids: Zondervan, 1980.

―――. *The Language of Love*. Waco, Tex.: Focus on the Family Publishing, 1988.

―――. *Love Is a Decision*. Dallas: Word, 1989.

Snyder, Chuch. *Incompatibility: Grounds for a Great Marriage*. Sisters, Ore.: Questar Publishers, 1988.

Thomas, David. *Households of Faith*. Washington, DC: U.S. Catholic Conference, 1979.

―――. *When God Is at Home with Your Family*. St. Meinrad, Ind.: Abbey Press, 1978.

van Balen Holt, Mary. *Marriage, A Covenant of Seasons*. Liguori: Liguori, 1992.

Urbine, William and William Seifert. *On Life and Love: A Guide to Catholic Teaching on Marriage and Family*. West Mystic, Conn.: Twenty-Third Publications, 1993.

Whitehead, Evelyn and James. *Christian Life Patterns*. New York: Image, 1982.

Wright, H. Norman. *Romancing Your Marriage*. Ventura, Calif.: Regal Books, 1987.

Zigler, Zig. *Courtship after Marriage*. Nashville: Thomas Nelson Publishers, 1990.

Divorce

Coyle, Hennessey, Bobbi. *Once More with Love: A Guide to Marrying Again*. Notre Dame: Ave Maria, 1993.

Fisher, Bruce. *When Your Relationship Ends*. San Luis Obispo, Calif.: Impact Publishers, 1992.

Medved, Diana. *The Case Against Divorce*. New York: Donald I. Fine Inc, 1989.

Richmond, Gary. *The Divorce Decision*. Word, 1988.

Ripple, Paula. *Growing Strong at Broken Places*. Notre Dame: Ave Maria, 1986.

Wallenstein, Judith. *Second Chances*. New York: Tickner and Fields, 1989.

Young, James. J., CSP. *Divorcing, Believing, Belonging*. New York: Paulist, 1984.

Stepfamilies

Cullen, Paul J. *Stepfamilies: A Catholic Guide*. Huntington, Ind.: Our Sunday Visitor Publishing, 1988.

Maddox, Brenda. *The Half Parent*. New York: M. Evans and Company, 1975.

Psychology

Calden, George. *I Count, You Count*. Niles, Ill.: Argus Communications, 1976.

Haney, William. *Communication and Organizational Behavior*. Homewood, Ill., Richard D. Irwin, Inc.: 1967.

Peck, M. Scott. *The Road Less Travelled*. New York: Simon and Schuster, 1978.

Journaling

Chapman, Joyce. *Journaling for Joy: Writing Your Way to Personal Growth and Freedom*. North Hollywood: Newcastle Publishing Company, 1991.

Kelsey, Morton. *Adventure Inward*. Minneapolis: Augsburg, 1980.

————. *The Other Side of Silence: A Guide to Christian Meditation.* New York: Paulist, 1976.

Smith, Margaret D. *Journal Keeper.* Grand Rapids: William Eerdmans Publishing Company, 1992.

Wakefield, Dan. *The Story of Your Life: Writing a Spiritual Autobiography.* Boston: Beacon Press, 1990.